LEON KIRCHNER

L.H.

FOR PIANO LEFT HAND

The first performance of this work was given by Leon Fleisher
December 6, 1995 at Carnegie Hall, New York City.

duration ca. 7 minutes

AMP 8209
First Printing: December 2005

ISBN 978-0-634-06750-1

Associated Music Publishers, Inc.

DISTRIBUTED BY

HAL•LEONARD®
CORPORATION
7777 W. BLUEMOUND RD. P.O. BOX 13819 MILWAUKEE, WI 53213

L.H.
for Leon Fleisher

Leon Kirchner

Tempo I

Meno mosso   *molto rapidomento*

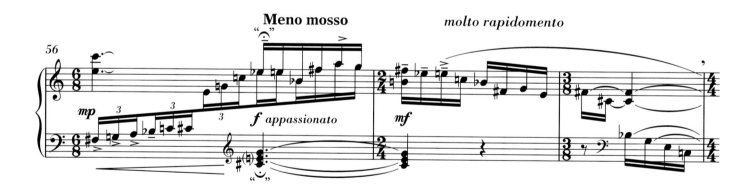

Poco Adagio   *gradually more violent and rapid*

slow down a bit

Tempo subito meno mosso *move ahead*

accel.

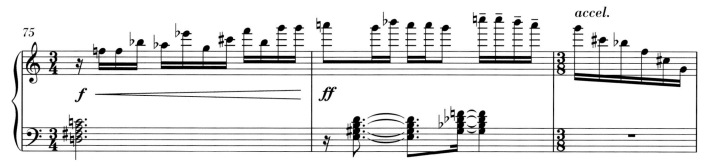

slow down poco a poco **Quasi Adagio** **Rapidamento**

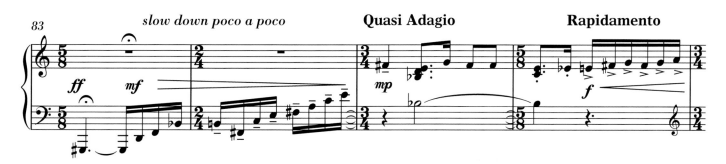

Tempo
meno mosso

Hold back

87

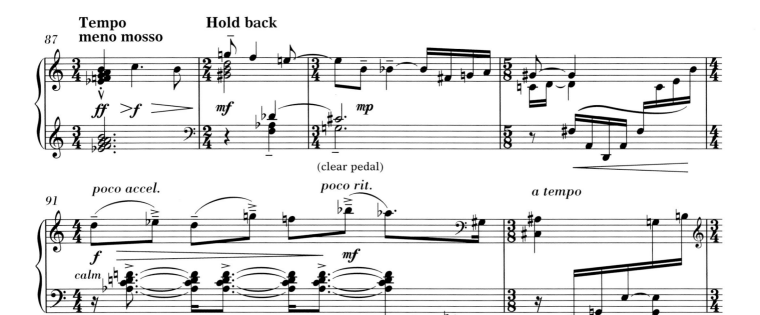

(clear pedal)

poco accel.

poco rit.

a tempo

91

93

96

99

102

a little forward